For Tara
<u>with love</u>

V.F.

Text copyright © 1991 by Vivian French
Illustrations copyright © 1991 by Jan Ormerod
First published in Great Britain by Walker Books Ltd

Printed and bound in Singapore by Tien Wah Press (PTE) Ltd.
First U.S. edition   1 2 3 4 5 6 7 8 9 10

Library of Congress Cataloging in Publication Data
French, Vivian. One ballerina two / written by Vivian French ; illustrated by Jan Ormerod.
p.   cm. Summary: Two young ballerinas practice their steps and movements.
ISBN 0-688-10333-2. — ISBN 0-688-10334-0 (lib. bdg.)   1. Ballet—Pictorial works—Juvenile
literature.   2. Ballerinas—Pictorial works—Juvenile literature.   [1. Ballet dancing.
2. Counting.]   I. Ormerod, Jan, ill.   II. Title.   III. Title: 1 ballerina 2. GV1787.5.F7
1991   792.8022'2—dc20   [E]
90-45969 CIP AC

One Ballerina Two

Written by Vivian French   Illustrated by Jan Ormerod

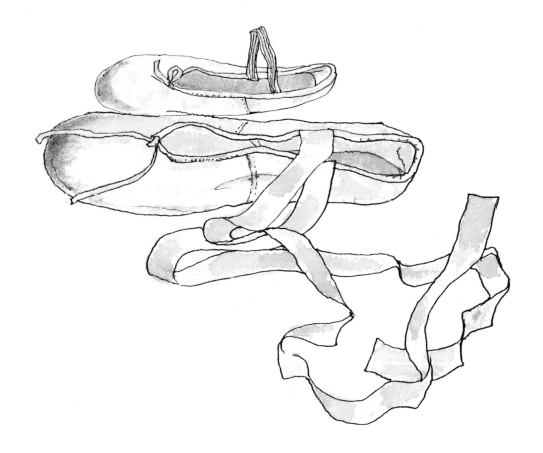

Lothrop, Lee & Shepard Books
New York

Ballerinas…

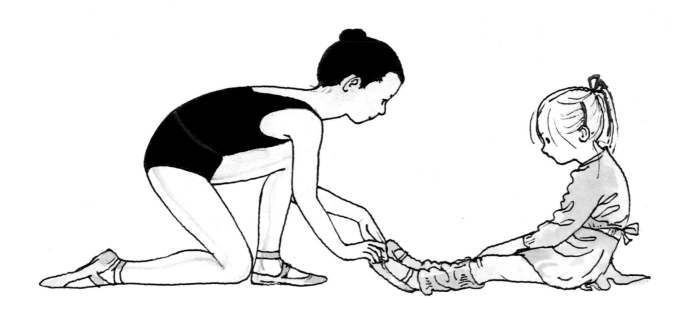

us two

10 Ten pliés

9 Nine knee bends

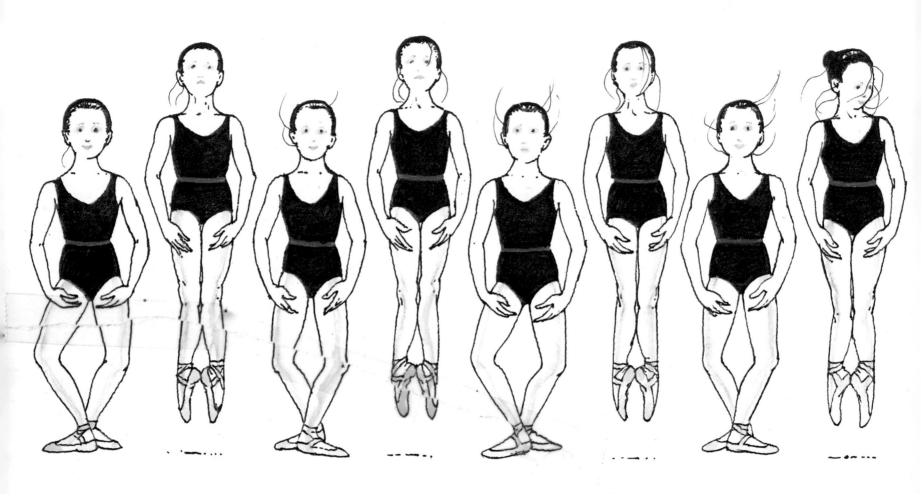

8 Eight changements

Seven little jumps

6 Six pirouettes

5 Five gallops

Oops!

4 Four pas de chat

3 Three pony trots

2 Two final curtsies

1 One happy hug

3

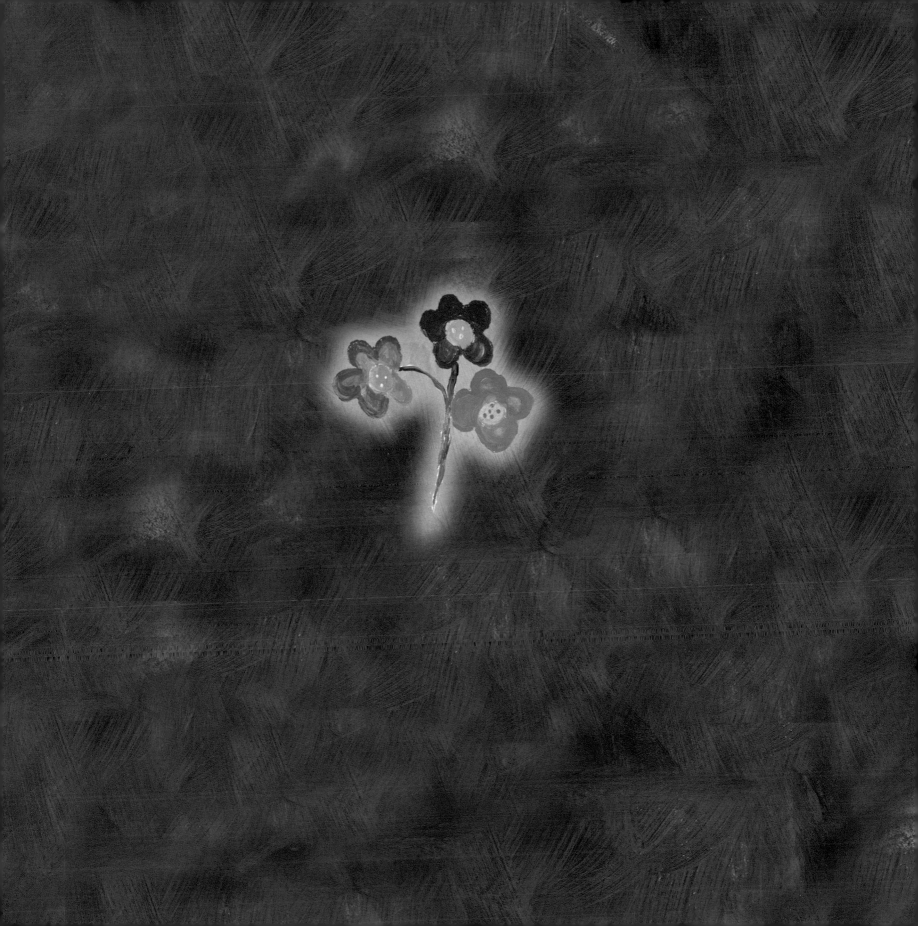

I Love You so Much...

is dedicated to

Cole James, Adam Jon, Julia Rose, and Will David,
who fill my heart with gigantic love. — MR

Library of Congress Control Number: 2007909082

Marianne Richmond Studios, Inc.
3900 Stinson Boulevard NE
Minneapolis, MN 55421
www.mariannerichmond.com

ISBN 10: 1-934082-26-0
ISBN 13: 978-1-934082-26-3

Illustrations by Marianne Richmond

Book design by Sara Dare Biscan

Printed in China

First Printing

Also available from author & illustrator
Marianne Richmond:

The Gift of an Angel
The Gift of a Memory
Hooray for You!
The Gifts of being Grand
I Love You So...
Dear Daughter
Dear Son
Dear Granddaughter
Dear Grandson
My Shoes take me Where I Want to Go
Fish Kisses and Gorilla Hugs
Happy Birthday to You!
I Wished for You, an adoption story
You are my Wish come True

Plus, she offers the *simply said...* and *smartly said...* mini book titles
for all occasions.

To learn more about Marianne's products,
please visit
www.mariannerichmond.com

I Love You so Much...

by

Marianne Richmond

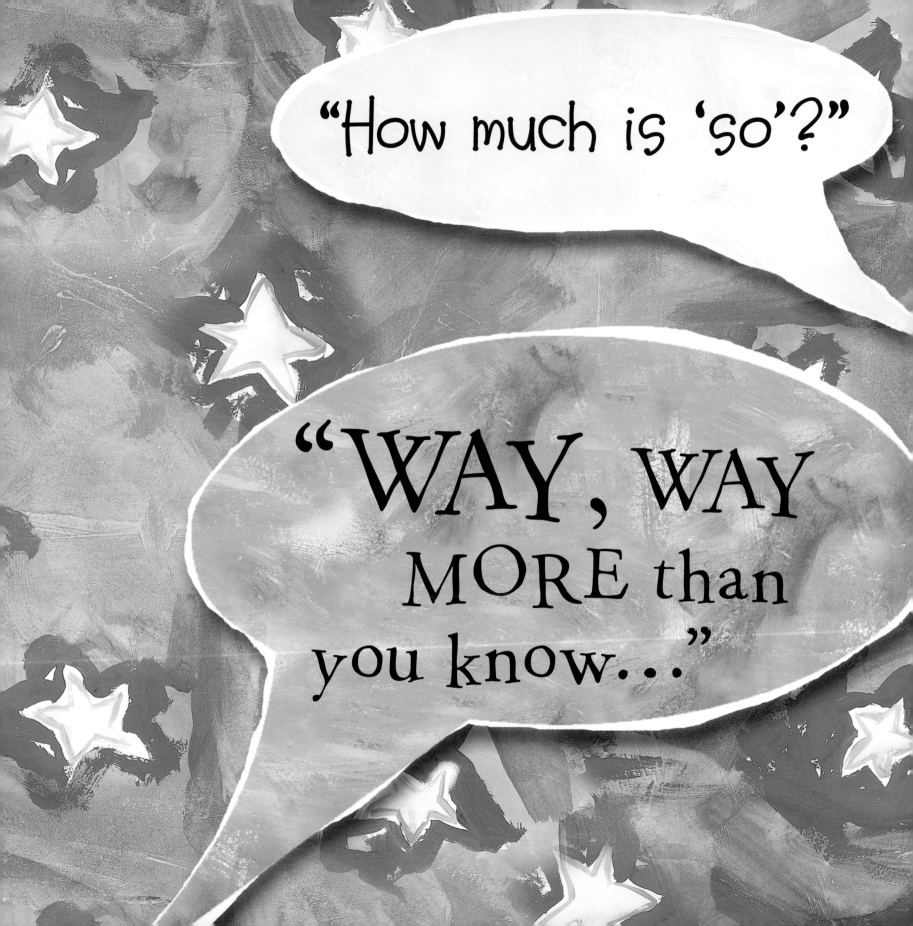

I love you as BRILLIANT
as each sparkling star,
and as WAY OUT as space,
I love you THAT far.

Marshmallows

I love you as GIGANTIC
as a great lion's roar,
and as DEEP as the ocean,
I love you MUCH more.

"That IS a lot," you say,
"but HOW did it start?
WHERE did love come from
to be in your heart?"

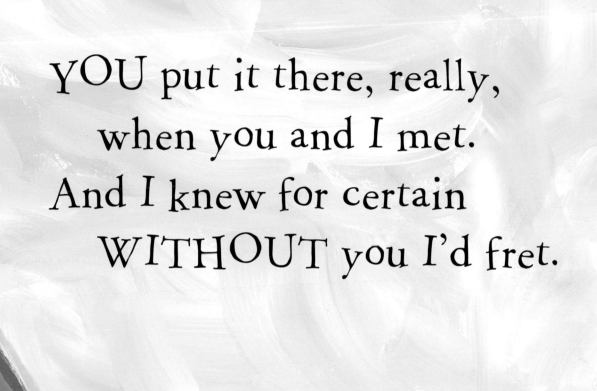

YOU put it there, really,
when you and I met.
And I knew for certain
WITHOUT you I'd fret.

From MY HEAD to my TOES,
I was feeling inside
a devotion for you
SO DEEP and SO WIDE.

And now it's ENORMOUS
and wonderfully real
and hard to describe
HOW MUCH I feel!

I love you as AWESOME
as a thundery sky,
and as SOARING as mountains,
I love you THAT high.

I love you as SILLY
as a puppy dog's kiss,
and as QUIET as midnight,
I love you like THIS.

I love you as STEADY
as the earth rounds the sun,
though SOME days of life
are the FARTHEST from fun.

"Like when you feel MAD?"
   you ask with distress,
"'cause I've BROKEN the rules
   or made a BIG mess?

Or, when I'm UNKIND,
   and your feelings are BLUE,
do you love me ALTHOUGH
   I do what I do?"

I love you being NICE,
and when you're CRANKY, too.
I love you without liking
the NAUGHTY things you do.

My 'love you' DOESN'T change like the temper of the days. It's a CERTAIN kind of thing in many DIFFERENT ways.

You're my SWEETIE, my dear,
my SMILE and laughter.

You're my PLAYMATE for always,
and my JOY ever after.

Hanging out WITH YOU
is where I want to be...
eating ice cream sundaes
or watching the TV.

UNDER your umbrella,
behind you on a bike.
BY you and BESIDE you
is what I REALLY like.

I love you NEAR or FAR.
I love you HIGH or LOW.
My love is there with you
WHEREVER you may go.

"Even when I'm SICK...
   and I can't get out of bed?
Do you love me better HEALTHY
   than with fever in my head?"

I love you sick or able.
You're ALWAYS you to me,
the ONE I LOVE forevermore.
Undeniably.

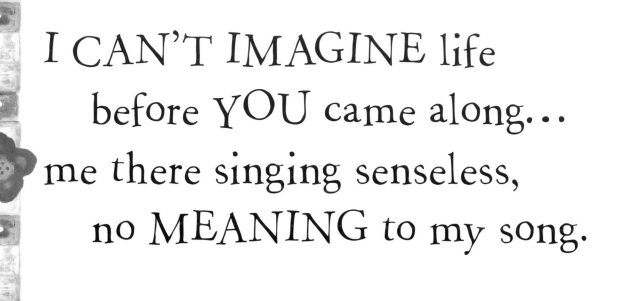

I CAN'T IMAGINE life
before YOU came along...
me there singing senseless,
no MEANING to my song.

Call it MEANT TO BE
or simply blessed fate,
you fill my heart WITH LOVE...
and for THAT I celebrate.

"WAY, WAY
MORE than
you know..."

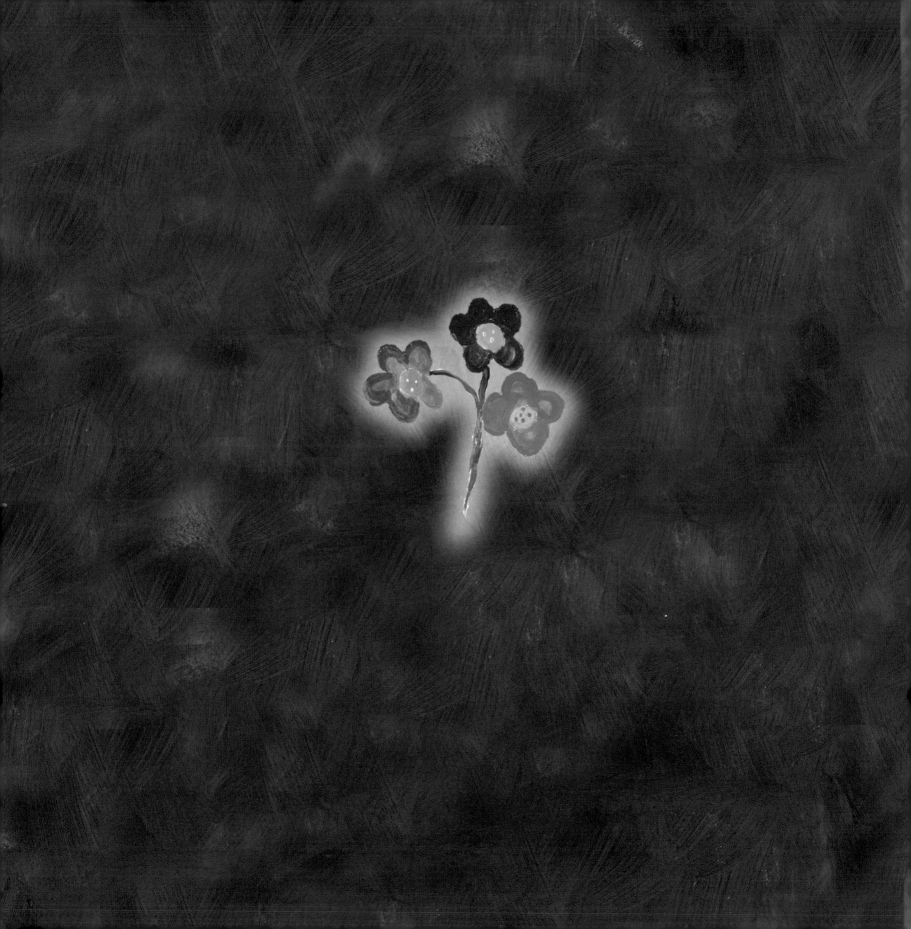